I READ IT ON THE REFRIGERATOR

Annette LaPlaca, *editor*

Harold Shaw Publishers
Wheaton, Illinois

Copyright © 1992 by Harold Shaw Publishers

Editor: Annette LaPlaca

Cover, design, & illustrations © 1992 by Turnbaugh & Associates

ISBN 0-87788-385-8

Library of Congress Cataloging-in-Publication Data

I read it on the refrigerator : memos for amazing moms / Annette LaPlaca, editor.
    p.   cm.
   Includes bibliographical references.
   ISBN 0-87788-385-8
   1. Mothers—Quotations, maxims, etc. 2. Motherhood—Quotations, maxims, etc. 3. Motherhood—Humor. I. LaPlaca, Annette Heinrich, 1964-
PN608.M6I2   1992
306.874'3—dc20   91-41656
                                                   CIP

99 98 97 96 95 94 93 92

10 9 8 7 6 5 4 3 2

CONTENTS

CELEBRATING MOTHERHOOD

What is a mother? To her child, she is everything—comfort, inspiration, security, example, identity, home. Celebrate God's excellent gift of the vocation of motherhood!

A mother is a mother still, the holiest thing alive. *Samuel Coleridge*

■

All that I am, or hope to be, I owe to my angel mother. *Abraham Lincoln*

■

Of all possible subjects upon which the artist can draw for inspiration, none has more universal appeal than that of mother and child. *Richard Gelb*

■

Super Moms were faster than a speeding bullet, more powerful than a harsh laxative, and able to leap six shopping carts on double stamp day. . . . She cut the grass, baked her own bread, shoveled the driveway, grew her own herbs, made the children's clothes, altered her husband's suits, played the organ at church, planned the vacation, paid the bills, was on three telephone committees, five car pools, two boards, took her ironing board down every week, stocked the freezer with sides of beef, made her own Christmas cards, voted in every election,

1

saw her dentist twice a year, assisted in the delivery of her dog's puppies, melted down old candles, saved the anti-freeze, and had a pencil by her telephone. *Erma Bombeck, The Grass Is Always Greener Over the Septic Tank*

■

To the man who has had a mother, all women are sacred for her sake. *Jean Paul Richter*

■

Motherhood . . . never questions age, height, religious preference, health, political affiliation, citizenship, morality, ethnic background, marital status, economic level, convenience, or previous experience. It's the biggest on-the-job training program in existence today. *Erma Bombeck*, Motherhood: The Second Oldest Profession

■

Mother had a strong and instinctive desire to play her role to the full. If she had been the queen of a court, she'd have started right in being regal and gracious, stirring up the lord chamberlain, and making sure the king toed the mark. *Clarence Day*, Life with Mother and Father

■

Richer than I you can never be
I had a mother who read to me.
Strickland Gillilan

■

God pardons like a mother, who kisses the offense into everlasting forgetfulness. *Jo Petty*, Apples of Gold

■

I missed being named Mother of the Year by three votes (all cast by my own children), I was not named to the Olympic Dusting Team, and I was laughed out of the Pillsbury Bake-off. *Erma Bombeck*, I Lost Everything in the Post-Natal Depression

■

A mother is not a person to lean on but a person to make leaning unnecessary. *Dorothy Canfield Fisher*, Her Son's Wife

■

It seems to me that my mother was the most splendid woman I ever knew. . . . I have met a lot of people knocking around the world since, but I have never met a more thoroughly refined woman than my mother. If I have amounted to anything, it will be due to her. *Charlie Chaplin*

■

A mother's prayers, silent and gentle, can never miss the road to the throne of all bounty. *Henry Ward Beecher*

■

When Mom gets chilly, everybody puts on a sweater, and when Mom gets tired, everybody takes a nap. . . . when Mom is on a diet, everybody starves. *Teresa Bloomingdale*, Sense and Momsense

■

The hand that rocks the cradle
Is the hand that rules the world.
W.R. Wallace

■

Perhaps a better woman after all,
With chubby children hanging on my neck
To keep me low and wise.
Elizabeth Barrett Browning

■

Mothers and teachers of children fill places so great that there isn't an angel in heaven that wouldn't be glad to give a bushel of diamonds to come down here and take their place. *Billy Sunday*

■

Parenthood remains the greatest single preserve of the amateur. *Alvin Toffler*, Future Shock

■

Anna Pearl Cosby brought up three boys with a husband in the Navy. I'm not going to talk long about my mother, but if I ever wanted a role model . . . it was Anna Pearl Cosby. *Bill Cosby, an interview*, Good Housekeeping

■

Instant availability without continuous presence is probably the best role a mother can play. *Lotte Bailyn*, The Woman in America

■

Mothering does have its many pleasurable moments, but those come only with a total commitment of the will to weather all the sticky times in between. *Stephen and Janet Bly*, How to Be a Good Mom

■

A mother is a person who sees that there are only four pieces of pie for five persons and promptly remarks that she's never cared for pie. *Unknown*

■

Mother knows best. *Anonymous*

■

I remember my mother's prayers—and they have always followed me. They have clung to me all my life. *Abraham Lincoln*

■

MOTHER'S OWN PRAYER

Now I lay me down to sleep
I pray the Lord nobody wakes me up.
If I should die before I wake
I wouldn't be surprised.
Betty Rollin, Mothers Are Funnier than Children

■

My mother came to all my performances. She'd lead the laughter and applause. If anybody spoke too loudly or coughed, my mother shushed them with an iron stare. *Milton Berle*

■

She is clothed with strength and dignity;
    she can laugh at the days to come. . . .
Her children arise and call her blessed;
    her husband also, and he praises her:
"Many women do noble things,
    but you surpass them all."
Proverbs 31:25, 28-29

■

Motherhood is a partnership with God. *Unknown*

■

In an obstetrician's office: "To heir is human." *Saturday Evening Post*

■

Others throw their faith away,
Mothers pray, and pray, and pray. *Amos R. Wells*

■

SQUEEZES

We love to squeeze bananas,
We love to squeeze ripe plums,
And when they are feeling sad
We love to squeeze our mums.
Brian Patten

■

What price success if one fails as a mother? *Mrs. Rosemary Foot*

■

Napoleon was once asked, "What is the greatest need of France?" His answer was, "Good mothers."

■

Being a mother is an excitement and enticement and a growth. *Dr. Beverly Raphael*

■

Youth fades; love droops; the leaves of friendship fall.
A mother's secret hope outlives them all. *Oliver Wendell Holmes*

■

Mothers, as well as fools, sometimes walk where angels fear to tread. *Unknown*

■

All that I am my mother made me. *John Quincy Adams*

■

My mother was the making of me. She was so true and so sure of me. I felt that I had someone to live for—someone I must not disappoint. The memory of my mother will always be a blessing to me. *Thomas A. Edison*

■

The precursor of the mirror is the mother's face.
D.W. Winnicott

■

That woman who is cool and collected, who is master of her countenance, her voice, her actions, and her gestures, will be the mother who is in control of her children, and who is greatly beloved by them. *Old Inscription*

■

The mother . . . the mysterious source of human life, where nature still receives the breath of God. *Pope Paul VI*

■

There was a place in childhood that I remember well,
And there a voice of sweetest tone bright fairy tales did tell.
Samuel Lover, "My Mother Dear"

■

Now that they're clean and tucked in bed,
It's angels that I see.
Can this really be the fiendish crew
That wrecked my house with glee?
Kathleen Cossaboom, in Good Housekeeping

■

There is no velvet so soft as mother's lap, no rose so
lovely as her smile, no path so flowery as that imprinted
with her footsteps. *Archbishop Thomsen*

■

He made the stars and gave them
Each an appointed place . . .
Created then, His masterpiece,
A mother's gentle face.
Mrs. Roy L. Peifer

■

A mother is a gardener—planting the seeds of faith, truth
and love that develop into the fairest flowers of character,
virtue and happiness in the lives of her children. *J. Harold
Gwynne*

■

To be a mother of men, a woman must make men of her
boys. She demands their best, not because it belongs to
her, but because it is due to them. For that which is due
children is not ease and luxury but hardening of muscles,

9

the habit of work, a sense of honor, and a self-respect born of integrity. *Unknown*

■

We mothers must recognize and accept a large portion of the responsibility of forming tomorrow's world. Let us plant so deeply in the hearts of our youth the seeds of tolerance and respect, of honor and integrity, that a better world will come . . . as a natural harvest of our own thoughtful planting. *Adeline Bullock*

■

At six weeks Baby grinned a grin
That spread from mouth to eyes to chin,
And Doc, the smartie, had the brass
To tell me it was only gas!
Margaret Fishbeck, Look Who's a Mother

■

The mother should consider herself as her child's sun, a changeless and ever-radiant world hither the small restless creature, quick at tears and laughter, light, fickle, passionate, full of storms, may come for fresh stores of light, warmth, and electricity, of calm and of courage. *Henri Amiel*

■

The sweetest sounds to mortals given
Are heard in Mother, Home, and Heaven.
William Goldsmith Brown

■

Being a mother is rewarding to one's female instincts, trying to one's nerves, physically exhausting, emotionally both frustrating and satisfying, and above all, *not* to be undertaken lightly. *Dr. Margaret Raphael*

■

Most of all the beautiful things in life come by twos or threes, by dozens and by hundreds. Plenty of roses, stars, sunsets, rainbows, brothers and sisters, aunts and cousins, but only one mother in the whole world. *Kate Douglas Wiggin*

■

Nothing can compare in beauty, and wonder, and admirableness, and divinity itself, to the silent work in obscure dwellings of faithful women bringing their children to honor and virtue and piety. *Henry Ward Beecher*

■

Never argue with Mother. She is logical enough, but the logic is entirely her own. . . . An accomplished motherly logician can hold two opposing ideas at the same time— and juggle them. *Betty Rollin,* Mothers Are Funnier Than Children

■

No man is poor who has a godly mother. *Abraham Lincoln*

■

A song of hope, a fervent prayer
A noble dream, and tender care;
A light of truth that makes me free—
All this my mother is to me. *J. Harold Gwynne*

■

A heart at peace with all the world,
Content with simple things . . .
She holds within her quiet rooms
The best that heaven brings.
Edna Jacques

■

All that I have ever accomplished in life, I owe to my mother. *Dwight L. Moody*

■

Her tender hands wrought for us before we entered the world. Her weary feet never failed to carry her at night to see that we were safe in dreamland. In the long, dark house, she watched and prayed. She shared our sorrows and gave us our joys. *Unknown*

■

Mighty is the force of Motherhood. *George Eliot*

■

There is one picture so beautiful that no painter has ever been able perfectly to reproduce it, and that is the picture of the mother holding in her arms her babe. *William Jennings Bryan*

■ ■ ■ ■ ■ ■ ■ ■ ■ ■ ■ ■ ■ ■ ■

CELEBRATING CHILDREN

Children—they fill our lives! We spend our days
celebrating the uniqueness of each one and
carefully safe-guarding these treasured gifts of a good God.

There is only one pretty child in the world, and every
mother has it! *J.C. Bridge*

■

He took a little child and had him stand among them.
Taking him in his arms, he said to them, "Whoever welcomes one of these little children in my name welcomes
me; and whoever welcomes me does not welcome me but
the one who sent me." *Mark 9:36-37*

■

Children are the anchors that hold a mother to life.
Sophocles

■

Children are gleeful barbarians. *Joseph Morgenstern*

■

God superintended your child's construction even down
to the tips of his fingers. And just as surely as that child
has his very own fingerprints, he has a lot of his very own
other things as well—personality, perspective, and
problems. He is as special as his fingerprints. *Cliff Schim-
mels*, Oh No! Maybe My Child Is Normal!

■

A little child born yesterday
A thing on mother's milk and kisses fed.
P.B. Shelley, "Homer's Hymn to Mercury"

■

The thing about having a baby—and I can't be the first
person to have noticed this—is that thereafter you *have* it,
and it's years before you can distract it from any elemen-
tal need by saying, "Oh, for heaven's sake, go look at
television!" *Jean Kerr*, Please Don't Eat the Daisies

■

Jesus said, "Let the little children come to me, and do not
hinder them, for the kingdom of heaven belongs to such
as these." *Matthew 19:14*

■

Children and bedtime—often two incompatible entities.
Vicki Huffman, Plus Living

■

Between the dark and the daylight,
When the night is beginning to lower,
Comes a pause in the day's occupations
That is known as the children's hour.
Henry Wadsworth Longfellow

■

Those of you who do not live around children may not
know what a Big Wheel is. It is a tricycle-like vehicle
made of plastic. When it is pedaled across pavement by a

four-year-old, it makes a sound unbearable to the adult ear. *Lewis Grizzard*, Kathy Sue Loudermilk, I Love You

■

Life is a flame that is always burning itself out, but it catches fire again every time a child is born. *George Bernard Shaw*

■

The sound of children laughing
Brightens up my day,
Gives me faith to journey onward,
And clears the skies of gray.
Dorothy W. Dial

■

It's an interesting fact that babies who won't smile for love or money will smile for vegetables. . . . A baby with a mouth full of strained spinach is almost guaranteed to smile from ear to ear, while green rivulets ooze down into his neck and all over his wrapper. *Jean Kerr*, How I Got to Be Perfect

■

It is not a slight thing when they, who are so fresh from God, love us. *Charles Dickens*

■

Children are children are children—and running, exploring, playing, climbing, and noisemaking just come with the territory.
Pamela Barden, in Parents and Children

■

There is so much that is beautiful and good to wake up to. Our children drive us toward this awakening. *Polly Berrien Berends*, Whole Child/Whole Parent

■

Let us look upon our children, let us love them and train them, as children of the covenant and children of the promise—these are the children of God. *Andrew Murray*, How to Raise Your Children for Christ

■

For the first two years of a child's life you try to get him to talk. For the next ten years you devote your life to getting him to shut up. For the remainder of his life you try to get his lips moving again and sound coming from his throat. *Erma Bombeck*, I Lost Everything in the Post-Natal Depression

■

I find nothing in this world more joyous than the spectacle of an almost brand-new infant (five months is about perfect) who has just been bathed and sprinkled with Johnson's baby powder and snapped into a clean pink wrapper with his gauzy hair swooshed up into a little peak. *Jean Kerr*, How I Got to Be Perfect

■

Of all people, children are the most imaginative. They abandon themselves without reserve to every illusion. *J.B. Macauley*

■

Kids are great. They are exciting. Their potential is simply phenomenal. And in any given family there is the potential to change this world for God. *Maxine Hancock*, Creative, Confident Children

■

Childhood is where "competition" is a baseball game and "responsibility" is a paper route. *Erma Bombeck*

■

God did not create a boring world. If we wonder at the uniqueness of a snowflake, how much more must we stand in awe of the infinite variety we find in human beings? Each child is more than an addition to the family. Through the gifts he or she brings, all family members are enriched. In a loving family, they all win. *Joseph and Lois Bird*, To Live as Family

■

Our children—even when smeared with mud or misdeeds—are God's gracious gift to us. *David Grant, "A Grace Assignment," in* Christian Parenting Today

■

Children are not so different from kites. . . . Children were created to fly. But they need wind—the undergirding and strength that comes from unconditional love, encouragement, and prayer. *Gigi Graham Tchividjian, "Catch the Wind," in* Christian Parenting Today

■

Every child comes with the message that God is not yet discouraged of man. *Tagore*

■

It's been my observation that as soon as a boy has become housebroken and a pleasure to have about, he is no longer about. He's in school all the time. *Jean Kerr,* How I Got to Be Perfect

■

God does not give bad gifts and good gifts; He simply gives different gifts. And when we can accept this in our children, we'll have come a long way toward understanding their uniqueness, and toward achieving family harmony. *Jay Kesler*, Ten Mistakes Parents Make with Teenagers

■

Adolescence is that period in a kid's life when his or her parents become more difficult. *Ryan O'Neal*

■

It will be worth the sacrifice, knowing you've done all you can to prepare your children to go out and make their way, on their own, in the Real World. Although they'll probably decide it's easier just to move back in with you. *Dave Barry,* Dave Barry Turns 40

■

When I was kidnapped, my parents snapped into action. They rented out my room. *Woody Allen*

■

Every child who comes into the world presents a new possibility for lifting the destiny of the human race. *Anna B. Mow*, Preparing Your Child to Love God

■

There are two classes of travel—first class and with children. *Robert Benchley*

■

Adolescence is the age at which children stop asking questions because they know all the answers. *Jo Petty,* Apples of Gold

■

We are responsible to God because our children are gifts from Him. There is no person alive—in or out of the womb—who is not a gift to his parents from God. It is impossible to comprehend the immense value of our lives and souls when we realize this one simple truth: We are all gifts from God. *Renee Jordan*, Parents, Love Your Children

■

Children are a great comfort in your old age—and they help you to reach it faster, too. *Lionel M. Kaufman*

■

Children aren't happy with nothing to ignore,
And that's what parents were created for.
Ogden Nash

■

A child more than all other gifts
That earth can offer to declining man
Brings hope with it, and forward-looking thoughts.
William Wordsworth

■

Every child born into the world is a new thought of
God, an ever-fresh and radiant possibility. *Kate Douglas
Wiggin*

■

A child is not a vase to be filled, but a lamp to be lighted.
Unknown

■

If you have lost your faith in yourself, just go out and get
acquainted with a small child. Win his love and your faith
will come stealing back to you before you know it. *Nick
Kenny*

■

Where children are, there is the golden age. *Novalis*

■

A baby is God's opinion that the world should go on.
Carl Sandburg

■

Children are God's small interpreters. *John Greenleaf
Whittier*

■

Children in a family are like flowers in a bouquet. There is always one determined to face in an opposite direction from the way the arranger desires. *Marcelene Cox, in* Oh No! Maybe My Child Is Normal!

■

A child is a most desirable pest. *Max Gralmich*

■

On the bright face of a child one can capture
The old hope and faith we would seek to redeem . . .
The beauty we once saw, the sweet childish rapture
In the eyes of a small child aglow with a dream. *Ruth B. Field*

■

The child, the seed, the grain of corn,
The acorn on the hill,
Each for some separate end is born
In season fit, and still
Each must in strength arise to work
The Almighty will. *Robert Louis Stevenson*

■

The children of today will be the architects of our country's destiny tomorrow.
James A. Garfield

■

Children today are tyrants. They contradict their parents, gobble their food, and tyrannize their teachers. *Socrates (470-399 B.C.)*

■

Pretty much all the honest truth-telling there is in the
world is done by children. *Oliver Wendell Holmes*

■

All mothers have their favorite child: the one who needs
you most at the moment—to cling to, to shout at, to hug,
to flatter, to unload on, to use . . . but mostly, to be there.
Erma Bombeck

■

There is this to be said about children. They keep you feeling old. *Jean Kerr*, How I Got to Be Perfect

■

Children are our most valuable natural resource. *Herbert
Hoover*

■

What I have no patience with is the growing tendency
among psychologists to insist that children are really
people, little adults—just like the rest of us, only
smaller. . . . We all know better than that. Children are different—mentally, physically, spiritually, quantitatively,
qualitatively, and furthermore they're all a little bit nuts.
Jean Kerr, Please Don't Eat the Daisies

■

What was wonderful about childhood is that anything
in it was a wonder. It was not merely a world full of
miracles, it was a miraculous world. *G.K. Chesterton*,
Autobiography

■

The one thing children wear out faster than shoes is parents. *John J. Plomp*

■

Most things have an escape clause . . . but children are forever. *Lewis Grizzard*, Chili Dawgs Always Bark at Night

■

Children are the only earthly possessions we can take with us to heaven. *Robert C. Savage*, Pocket Quips

■ ■ ■ ■ ■ ■ ■ ■ ■ ■ ■ ■ ■ ■ ■ ■

THE HARDEST JOB YOU'LL EVER LOVE

One parent calls motherhood "the hardest job you'll ever
love." And you know from personal experience
that building a positive family environment
for children is almost as exhausting as it is rewarding!

Motherhood is like the Peace Corps—it's the hardest job
you'll ever love. *Judy Watts Breckenridge, in* Good Housekeeping

■

The Lord was wise enough to make a woman's pregnancy
last nine months. If it were shorter, people with temporary
insanity might have two or three kids a year. *Bill Cosby*,
Fatherhood

■

It is not uncommon for a mother, particularly, to feel over-
whelmed by the complexity of her parental assignment.
For each child she raises, she is the primary protector of
his health, education, intellect, personality, character, and
emotional stability. She must serve as physician, nurse,
psychologist, teacher, minister, cook, and policeman.
James Dobson, Dare to Discipline

■

Parents have a job that requires lots of experience to per-
form and none at all to get. *Unknown*

■

I'll tell you how bad I was at diapering. My four kids potty-trained themselves as soon as they could walk because it was so difficult to get around with all that drapery around their ankles. *Margery Eliscu*, Roger Baker, Erma Bombeck and Me

■

Mothers measure out their lives in dirty dishes. No matter how many times a day we clean up the kitchen, dirty dishes continue to sprout around us, unbidden, unwanted, and unclaimed. *Teresa Bloomingdale,* Sense and Momsense

■

Just about the time you think you can make both ends meet, somebody moves the ends. *Pansy Penner*

■

Mother—that was the bank where we deposited all our hurts and worries. *DeWitt Talmage*

■

He who laughs, lasts. *Mary Pettibone Poole*

■

Lord
Not for a single moment
Could I make it
Down here
If you did not intercede for me
Up there.
Ruth Harms Calkin, "Factual," in Lord, I Keep Running Back to You

■

The best way to clean a frying pan that has burned food cemented to the bottom is to let it soak in soapy water for several days and then, when nobody is looking, throw it in the garbage. *Dave Barry,* Homes and Other Black Holes

■

Insanity is hereditary. You get it from your kids. *Unknown*

■

A baby is an inestimable blessing and bother. *Mark Twain*

■

Do not, on a rainy day, ask your child what he feels like doing, because I assure you that what he feels like doing you won't feel like watching. *Fran Lebowitz*, Social Studies

■

I will never understand children. I never pretended to. *Erma Bombeck*, If Life Is a Bowl of Cherries, What Am I Doing in the Pits?

■

I used to be a reasonably careless and adventurous person before I had children: now I am morbidly obsessed by seatbelts and constantly afraid that low-flying aircraft will drop on my children's school. *Margaret Drabble*

■

Babysitters are girls you hire to watch your television set. *Unknown*

■

Our theory is, if there is nobody besides ourselves around to see the dirt, then the dirt isn't really there. So Rule Number One of successful housecleaning is: Never Let Anybody into Your House. . . . Rule Number Two of successful housecleaning, of course, is: Never Have Children of Any Kind. *Dave Barry*, Homes and Other Black Holes

■

Life is full of interruptions, emergencies, crises, and urgent happenings. A mother must train herself to go with the flow. *Pat Holt and Grace Ketterman*, Choices Are Not Child's Play

■

The definition of perfect parenting
   is easy to express,
Just err and err and err again
   but less and less and less.
Kay Kuzma, A Hug and a Kiss and a Kick in the Pants

■

Ask your child what he wants for dinner only if he's buying. *Fran Lebowitz*, Social Studies

■

The best time for parents to put the children to bed is while they still have the strength. *Homer Phillips*

■

Learning to live with your family begins with a realistic view of its possibilities and its problems.
Eugene Kennedy

■

You'd better believe that I'm never too busy for my children. I *absolutely* have time for them. *Barbara Bush*

■

A masterpiece my toddler drew
With strokes so bold and tall,
And colors blended artfully—
Too bad it's on the wall!
Patricia Elizabeth Garner, in Good Housekeeping

■

It's important to cultivate a sense of serving one another
at home. The place where you live is the place where you
will have the most opportunities to serve the Lord by serving others. *Annette LaPlaca*, Making Summer Count

■

No one knows what her life expectancy is, but I have a
horror of leaving this world and not having anyone in the
entire family know how to replace a toilet tissue spindle.
Erma Bombeck, If Life Is a Bowl of Cherries, What Am I Doing in
the Pits?

■

By the time a family gets the suitcases packed and the car
loaded, they need a vacation! *Unknown*

■

There was no need to do any housework at all. After the first
four years, the dirt doesn't get any worse. *Quentin Crisp*

■

Not only is woman's work never done, the definition keeps
changing. *Bill Copeland, in* Herald-Tribune (Sarasota, Florida)

∎

To be patient in little things, to be tolerant in large affairs, to be happy in the midst of petty cares and monotonies, that is wisdom. *Joseph Fort Newton*

∎

Help your children remember that even the most everyday activities are part of serving the Lord. You will model this serving mentality by practicing kindness—a sympathetic word to the young man who is pumping your gas during a thunderstorm, cheerful patience in the face of a rude salesclerk, a cold Coca-cola for the woman mowing the apartment lawn, a brownie for the tired UPS delivery man. . . . Each loving act says loud and clear, "I love you. God loves you. I care. God cares." *Joyce Heinrich and Annette LaPlaca*, Making Summer Count

∎

Fingerprinting children is a good idea. It will settle the question as to who used the guest towel in the bathroom. *Unknown*

∎

Have you taken time lately to thank God for these wonderful gifts you call your children? Or has life been so busy that you see them only as challenges, as mischiefs, as time eaters, as heavy responsibilities, or as headaches and problems? *Tim Hansel*, What Kids Need Most in a Dad

∎

Service is love in working clothes. *Keith L. Brooks*, The Cream Book: Sentence Sermons

■

Cleaning your house while your kids are still growing is like shoveling the walk before it stops snowing. *Phyllis Diller*

■

The highest of distinctions is service to others. *King George VI*

■

People who say they sleep like a baby usually don't have one. *Leo Burke*

■

Lord, the newness of this day
Calls me to an untried way:
Let me gladly take the road,
Give me strength to bear my load,
Thou my guide and helper be—
I will travel through with Thee.
Henry van Dyke

■

Having a family is like having a bowling alley installed in your brain. *Martin Mull*

■

My mother had a great deal of trouble with me, but I think she enjoyed it. *Mark Twain*

■

Life is either a daring adventure or nothing at all. *Helen Keller*

■

If your child draws pictures of cows on your woodwork with a felt-tipped marker, you can scrub them with a mixture of one part baking soda, one part lemon juice, and one part ammonia, but they won't come off. *Dave Barry, Homes and Other Black Holes*

■

I hate housework! You make the beds, you do the dishes— and six months later you have to start all over again. *Joan Rivers*

■

Some may climb Mount Everest in search of thrills
   galore,
But I scale peaks that rival it just past my laundry door.
Slopes of socks and underwear, sheer cliffs of shirts and
   pants—
Oh yes, I live in mortal fear of a laundry avalanche.
Maggie Thurmond, "Of Detergent and Determination," in Ladies Home Journal

■

I love the word impossible. *Ann Kiemel*

■

Small children have no concept whatsoever of cleanliness. A small child's concept of housekeeping is to lick spilled pudding off the living room carpet. *Dave Barry,* Homes and Other Black Holes

■

Educational television should be absolutely forbidden. It can only lead to unreasonable expectations and eventual disappointment when your child discovers that the letters of the alphabet do not leap up out of books and dance around the room with royal-blue chickens. *Fran Lebowitz*, Social Studies

■

There is nothing wrong with the world that a sensible woman could not settle in an afternoon. *Jean Giraudaux*

■

If there is one child and one toy, the child plays with the toy and makes no fuss about it. If there are two children and one toy there is a fight which has to be arbitrated by everybody in the house, including the cook, the yardman, and the woman who comes in on Tuesdays to iron. *Harold H. Martin*, Father's Day Comes Once a Year—and Then It Rains

■

WAIT

These are
the good
old days.
Just wait
and see. *Steve Turner*, Up-to-Date

■

Drop thy still dews of quietness
   Till all our strivings cease;
Take from our souls the strain and stress
   And let our ordered lives confess
   The beauty of Thy peace.

John Greenleaf Whittier

■ ■ ■ ■ ■ ■ ■ ■ ■ ■ ■ ■ ■ ■ ■ ■

TRAIN·UP·A·CHILD

Guiding your children into responsible, godly adulthood
is the most important work of your life.
Pray for wisdom as you seek to train your children.

Train a child in the way he should go, and when he is old
he will not turn from it. *Proverbs 22:6*

God is always our model and source for becoming positive parents. *Don Highlander,* Positive Parenting

She speaks with wisdom,
    and faithful instruction is on her tongue.
Proverbs 31:26

The mother's heart is the child's schoolroom. *Henry Ward Beecher*

The bearing and training of a child
Is woman's wisdom. *Alfred Lord Tennyson, "Princess"*

American wives and American mothers, as surely as "the
hand that rocks the cradle is the hand that rules the
world," have, through their nurture of children and their

influence over men, the destinies of our Nation in their
keeping to a greater extent than any other single agency.
Grover Cleveland

Raising kids is part joy and part guerilla warfare. *Ed Asner*

Before I got married I had six theories about bringing up
children; now I have six children and no theories. *Lord
Rochester*

■

Love and discipline are the foundation of training your child. Love is essential from infancy through growing years. It would be difficult for your child to become a happy, emotionally secure person without generous amounts of love! Without discipline you can not hope to teach your child to be a respectful, competent, and responsible adult.   *J. Allen Peterson*, Two Become One

■

Capturing the teachable moment is essential for teaching spiritual truths and values. . . . Our children learn so easily, so happily when the lesson is a natural part of conversation, an answer to a question, or an overflow of our own hearts shared with them.   *Joyce Heinrich*, Making Summer Count

■

Train is a word of deep importance for every parent to understand. Training is not telling, not teaching, not commanding, but something higher than all these. It is not only *telling* a child what to do, but also *showing him how to do it* and seeing that it is *done*.   *Andrew Murray*, How to Raise Your Children for Christ

■

The worst thing you can do when reprimanding children is to indicate the nature and the degree of your desperation. . . . you accomplish nothing by throwing yourself on their mercy and asking piteously, "Are you trying to drive your poor mommy smack out of her mind?" Of course

they are, but do you think they'll admit it? *Jean Kerr,*
Please Don't Eat the Daisies

■

Each child is unique, a special creation of God with
talents, abilities, personality, preferences, dislikes, poten-
tials, strengths, weaknesses, and skills that are his or her
own. As parents, we must seek to identify these in each of
our children and help them become the persons God
intended. *Dave Veerman, in* Parents and Children

■

There's no substitute for the sense of satisfaction that
comes from watching as your children, under your steady,
guiding hand, develop from tiny, helpless Frequent Barfer
modules into full-grown, self-reliant young adults fully
capable of crashing your car into a day-care center. *Dave*
Barry, Dave Barry Turns 40

■

To show a child what has once delighted you, to find the
child's delight added to your own, so that there is now a
double delight seen in the glow of trust and affection, this
is happiness. *J.B. Priestly*

■

Raising children is a creative endeavor, an art rather than
a science. *Bruno Bettelheim,* A Good Enough Parent

■

Babies come into the world with no instructions, and you
pretty much have to assemble them on your own. They

are maddeningly complex, and there are no guaranteed formulas that work in every instance. *James Dobson*, Parenting Isn't for Cowards

∎

To us as parents is entrusted the vital task of character development—of imprinting the distinctive stamp of godliness upon the lives of our children. *Maxine Hancock*, Creative, Confident Children

∎

The best parenting skills come most naturally when the parents are on their knees. *Julie Bakke*

∎

Folly is bound up in the heart of a child,
   but the rod of discipline will drive it far from him. . . .
The rod of correction imparts wisdom,
   but a child left to himself disgraces his mother.
Proverbs 22:15; 29:15

∎

When we train our children, we initiate techniques that bring about a submissive will. We also discover ways to develop our child's taste so that he delights in things that are wholesome and right. None of this is naturally known by a child. These are things parents need to inculcate during those growing-up years in the home. *Charles R. Swindoll*, You and Your Child

■

Training a child is more or less a matter of pot luck. *Rod Maclean*

■

Prime-time parents are parents who consider every minute with their children prime time to communicate the message of parental love, interest, and care. *Kay Kuzma*, Prime-Time Parenting

■

If you are going to do anything permanent for the average man, you must begin before he is a man. *Theodore Roosevelt*

■

In spite of six thousand manuals on child raising in the bookstores, child raising is still a dark continent and no one really knows anything. You just need a lot of love and luck—and, of course, courage because you'll be spending years in fear of your kids. *Bill Cosby*, Fatherhood

■

Self-esteem isn't a lesson you teach; it's a quality you nurture. *Dr. Ronald Levant and John Kelly*, Between Father and Child

■

When you listen to your children, you are paying them a compliment. By listening, you increase their feelings of self-respect and self-worth. *Dean and Grace Merrill*, Together at Home

■

Only be careful, and watch yourselves closely so that you do not forget the things your eyes have seen or let them slip from your heart as long as you live. Teach them to your children and to their children after them.   *Deuteronomy 4:9*

■

The training of children is a profession where we must know how to lose time in order to gain it.   *Rousseau*

■

Parents who devote time to their children . . . will perceive in them subtle needs for discipline, to which they will respond with gentle urging or reprimand or structure or praise, administered with thoughtfulness and care. . . . They will take the time to make these minor corrections and adjustments, listening to their children, responding to them, tightening a little here, loosening a little there, giving them little lectures, little stories, little hugs and kisses, little admonishments, little pats on the back.
M. Scott Peck, The Road Less Traveled

■

Love the LORD your God with all your heart and with all your soul and with all your strength. These commandments that I give you today are to be upon your hearts. Impress them on your children. Talk about them when you sit at home and when you walk along the road, when you lie down and when you get up.   *Deuteronomy 6:5-7*

■

If a child lives with friendliness he learns that the world is a nice place in which to live.   *Unknown*

■

If it is desirable that children be kind, appreciative, and pleasant, those qualities should be taught—not hoped for. If we want to see honesty, truthfulness, and unselfishness in our offspring, then these characteristics should be conscious objectives of our early instructional process.   *James Dobson*, Dare to Discipline

■

The hardest part of raising children is teaching them to ride bicycles. . . . A shaky child on a bicycle for the first time needs both support and freedom. The realization that this is what the child will always need can hit hard.   *Sloan Wilson*

■

As I take God's view of my children, I see them being formed into his image and receive it as a finished matter. I have seen the end from the middle and the matter is settled.   *Jack Taylor*, One Home Under God

■

We need to expose our children to aggressive, vital, dynamic Christianity and continue to pray for them. Prayer accomplishes more than anything else.   *Bill Bright, in* How to Raise Christian Kids in a Non-Christian World

■

Interest your kids in bowling. Get them off the streets and into the alleys. *Don Rickles*

■

In praising or loving a child we love and praise not that which is, but that which we hope for. *Goethe*

■

We reap what we sow, more than we sow, later than we sow. *Charles Stanley*

■

If you bungle raising your children, I don't think whatever else you do well matters very much. *Jacquelyn Kennedy*

■

It is better to keep children to their duty by a sense of honor and by kindness than by fear. *Terence*

■

Character is not something highly valued in this society. Our children will get little or no reinforcement for having strong character outside the home, so it is most important that the development of strong character be emphasized and rewarded in the home. *Charles Stanley*, How to Keep Your Kids on Your Team

■

You don't raise heroes; you raise sons. And if you treat them like sons, they'll turn out to be heroes, even if it's just in your own eyes. *Walter Schirra, Sr.*

Some parents bring up their children on thunder and lightning, but thunder and lightning never yet made anything grow. Rain or sunshine cause growth—quiet penetrating forces that develop life. *Unknown*

■

The middle ground of love and control must be sought if we are to produce healthy, responsible children. *James Dobson*, Dare to Discipline

■

The most influential of educational factors is the conversation in a child's home. *William Temple*

■

We should strive to produce responsible adults who are able to function independently of parents' authority, yet wholly submitted to God's. If all goes well, they should become adults who live directly responsible to God within the limitations He has ordained. *Charles Stanley*, How to Keep Your Kids on Your Team

■

Place before children nothing but what is simple, lest you spoil the taste—and nothing that is not innocent, lest you spoil the heart. *Joseph Joubet*

■

Do not withhold discipline from a child;
  if you punish him with the rod, he will not die.
Punish him with the rod
  and save his soul from death.
Proverbs 23:13-14

■

Because we love our children we should be patient with them. Just think how patient God is with us. How He waits in love until we decide to come to Him. . . . How He tolerates again and again our sinning and is joyful when we ask to be forgiven! How tirelessly He listens to our excuses . . . watches our stumbling feet so that He can catch us when we fall! Our Heavenly Father never says, "I told you so!" Instead He sets us back on our feet with tender, loving hands. How precious is the patience of the Lord, and how endless His mercies! We need to be patient with our children in the same way God is patient with us. *Renee Jordan*, Parents, Love Your Children

■

The child that never learns to obey his parents in the home
will not obey God or man out of the home. *Susanna Wesley*

■

Your child is watching too much television if there exists the
possibility that he might melt down. *Fran Lebowitz,* Social Studies

■

Let parents bequeath to their children not riches, but the
spirit of reverence. *Plato*

■

Let love be your guide! A relationship that is charac-
terized by genuine love and affection is likely to be a
healthy one, even though some parental mistakes and
errors are inevitable. *James Dobson,* The Strong-Willed Child

■

Teach your child to hold his tongue. He'll learn fast
enough to speak. *Benjamin Franklin*

■

Women who fulfill their vocation hold power even over
powerful men; such women mold public opinion and
prepare future generations. And so it is they who hold the
power to save people from all our present and impending
evils. Yes, women, mothers, in your hands more than in
those of anyone else, lies the salvation of the world. *Leo
Tolstoy,* The Lion and the Honeycomb

■ ■ ■ ■ ■ ■ ■ ■ ■ ■ ■ ■ ■ ■ ■

MOTHERLOVE

Nothing quite matches the unique affection and strong
bond between mother and child. Of all the
types of love people experience in their lifetimes,
motherlove–being the first–may be the most important.

Mother Love enfolds the heart and gives it dreams to sing.
Virginia Covey Boswell

■

Mother love is mighty benefaction
The prop of the world and its population
If mother love died the world would rue it
No money would bring the women to it. *Stevie Smith*

■

Love isn't just happiness in ideal situations with everything going according to daydreams of family life or married life or parent-child closeness and confidence. Love
has *work* to do! Hard and self-sacrificial work. *Edith
Schaeffer,* What Is a Family?

■

Parenthood is just the world's most intensive course in
love. *Polly Berrien Berends*, Whole Child/Whole Parent

■

There's nothing more precious
Than a mother's sweet prayer.

There's nothing more gracious
Than the love she will share.
There's nothing as strong
As the faith she declares;
And when things go wrong
We know that she cares.
Clay Harrison

■

Love is patient, love is kind . . . it is not self-seeking, it is
not easily angered, it keeps no record of wrongs . . . It
always protects, always trusts, always hopes, always per-
severes. Love never fails. *1 Corinthians 13:4-8*

■

Whether she be eighteen or eighty, Mother is an irreplace-
able treasure. None other will ever love you half so well
or half so foolishly. None other will be so sure you are
right, good, and worthy. Of course, sometimes she is
wrong, but God love her for it and keep her forever in His
grace. *Alan Beck, in* Especially for Mothers

■

Mother's love is a precious thing
That deepens through the years,
In memory of bright sunshine days,
Of laughter, love, and tears.
Mother's love is a treasured thing;
Though far from home we roam,
The cherished bonds of faith and love
Still pull our hearts toward home. *Elisabeth Weaver Winstead*

■

One lamp, thy mother's love, amid the stars shall lift its pure flame changeless, and before the throne of God burn through eternity. *A.P. Willis*

■

Unconditional love is loving a child no matter what. No matter what the child looks like. No matter what his assets, liabilities, handicaps. No matter what we expect him to be, and most difficult, no matter how he acts. *Ross Campbell*, How to Really Love Your Child

■

In all this cold and hollow world, no fount
Of deep, strong, deathless love, save that within
A mother's heart.
Felicia Hemans

■

No language can express the power and beauty and heroism and majesty of a mother's love. It . . . sends the radiance of its quenchless fidelity like a star in heaven. *Edwin H. Chapin*

■

A mother's heart is always with her children. *German proverb*

■

Children desperately need to know—and to hear in ways they understand and remember—that they're loved and valued by Mom and Dad. *Gary Smalley and Paul Trent*, The Language of Love

■

Lord, give the mothers of the world
　　More love to do their part;
That love which reaches not alone
The children made by birth their own,
　　But every childish heart.
Wake in their souls true motherhood,
Which aims at universal good.
Ella Wheeler Wilcox

■

The only authority that has an intrinsic right to be obeyed
is the authority of a great love for our children that will
express and commend to them the greater love of the
Heavenly Father. *Thomas Small*, The Forgotten Father

■

Hearts will never be practical until they can be made
unbreakable. *Frank Baum*, The Wizard of Oz

■

The first, most fundamental right of childhood is the
right to be loved. The child comes into the world
alone, defenseless, without resource. Only love can
stand between his infant helplessness and the savagery
of a harsh world. *Paul Hanly Furfey*, The Church and the
Child

■

My mother loved children—she would have given anything if I'd been one. *Groucho Marx*

■

Love must be tough. *James Dobson*

■

You can give birth to a child, nurse the child, clothe, feed, discipline, and educate that child—without really knowing the one you are raising. . . . Knowing your child is primary. Loving your child requires knowing that child. *Charles R. Swindoll*, You and Your Child

■

Children need love, especially when they do not deserve it. *Harold S. Hulbert*

■

Romance fails us
and so do friendships
but the relationship of
Mother and Child
remains indelible and indestructible
the strongest bond upon the earth.
Theodore Reik

■

I had a mother once, who cared for me with such passionate regard, who loved me so intensely, that no language can describe the yearning of her soul. *William Lloyd Garrison*

■

Mother is a word called Love. *Helen Steiner Rice*

■

In his mother's heart no baby ever grows up completely, and in some mysterious fashion a part of every man remains a child, peculiarly his mother's. *Dame Enid Lyons*

■

Mothers' arms are made of tenderness, and sweet sleep blesses the child who lies therein. *Victor Hugo*

■

In this wintry world, it is a tender mother's love and a pious mother's care that are the carpet on the floor and the blaze on the hearth of every home. *Keith L. Brooks*, The Cream Book: Sentence Sermons

■

No language can express the power and beauty and heroism of a mother's love. *Edwin H. Chapin*

■

The angels, whispering to one another, can find, among their burning terms of love, none so devotional as that of "Mother." *Edgar Allan Poe*

■

Mothers are the angels sent by God to touch our lives with the light and the warmth of His caring. Through their guidance, we seek and find the path to our future. By their inspiration we make our own contribution to life and posterity. *Edith Schaffer Lederberg*

■

If a parent neglects to give a child love, no one else can substitute for that gap. The child will suffer. Parental love is of primary importance. . . . A parent can never give too much love to a child. *Kay Kuzma*, Prime-Time Parenting

■

No woman who has not experienced the mixed blessings of motherhood, could possibly imagine the strength of the tie between a mother and her children. *Priscilla Kincaid-Smith*

■

Who is it that loves me and will love me forever with an affection which no chance, no misery, no crime of mine can do away? It is you, my mother. *Thomas Carlyle*

■

If there be aught surpassing human deed or word or thought, it is a mother's love. *Marchioness de Spadara*

■

Mother means selfless devotion, limitless sacrifice, and love that passes understanding. *Unknown*

■ ■ ■ ■ ■ ■ ■ ■ ■ ■ ■ ■ ■ ■ ■

JUST LIKE YOU, MOM

Part of a mother's role is to be a model of Christian
life in the world—a role loaded with
responsibility. Seek Christ's help to meet this challenge.

Be that yourself which you would bring others to be. Be it
with your whole being. . . . the power of example in a
parent does more to train a child than any other single
thing. *Larry Christenson*, The Christian Family

Worship involves more than attending church or handing
out tracts. It means doing the best you can at whatever
you are doing, and being the best person you can be. We
are commanded to let our lights shine before men, and
there are many ways we can do that. Parents should make
sure their lights shine at home. *John Whitehead, in* How to
Raise Christian Kids in a Non-Christian World

Values are not *taught* to our children, they are *caught* by
them. *Unknown*

Any child will learn to worship God who lives his daily
life with adults who worship Him. *Anna B. Mow*, Preparing
Your Child to Love God

■

I am nothing like my mother. Really. . . . I am nothing
like my mother. Honest. . . . I am nothing like my
mother. We come from two different worlds. . . . All I
have to give her is admiration for the most courageous
woman I have ever known, respect for the wisest
human being I have ever met, and love for the most
beautiful face I will ever see. I am nothing like my
mother. I wish I were.   *Erma Bombeck, in* Good Housekeeping

■

Satisfaction comes from having a lasting, positive im-
pact on the lives of others. Nobody on earth even
comes close to a mother for having the potential for
that kind of influence.   *Stephen and Janet Bly*, How to Be a
Good Mom

■

Children have more need of models than of critics.   *Joseph
Joubert*

■

An ounce of loving role modeling is worth a pound of
parental pressure.   *V. Gilbert Beers, in* How to Raise Christian
Kids in a Non-Christian World

■

Childhood is like a mirror, which reflects in after life the
images first presented to it.   *Samuel Smiles*

Don't worry that your children never listen to you; worry
that they are always watching you.   *Robert Fulghum*

■

There is never much trouble in any family where the children hope someday to resemble their parents. *William Lyon Phelps*

■

The best way to teach character is to have it around the house. *Unknown*

■

There is something in parenting that is more than principles. You may buy every book about parenting, catalog every principle, memorize the list, and even do your best to put these principles into your child's life. But there is something lost in translation unless principles become flesh and blood, heart and mind, and live themselves out in your life. *V. Gilbert Beers, in* How to Raise Christian Kids in a Non-Christian World

■

A child's relationship to Jesus thrives in direct relation to the obedience he gives to his parents. *Larry Christenson,* The Christian Family

■

My parents showed me a lot about a gracious God. As a result, viewing God as a loving Parent hasn't been a difficult task. To me he is a God who, like my parents, not only has great expectations but who understands my limitations and readily gives needed encouragement. *Jean Sheldon*

■

If a child lives with acceptance and friendship,
  He learns to find love in the world.
Dorothy Law Nolte

■

One of the greatest desires children have is to grow up to
be like Mom and Dad. Each new skill they learn, each
new place they experience, each new phrase or word they
define is a building block to maturity, and children instinc-
tively know it. *Joyce Heinrich*, Making Summer Count

■

Children are natural mimics—they act like their parents
in spite of every attempt to teach them good manners.
Unknown

■

Our children observe us all day long, at our best and at our
worst. They try to follow in our footsteps, copying and
mimicking us from the very beginning of their tender lives.
Much of what they learn comes simply from living with us
and observing us. *Shirley Suderman, in* Parents and Children

■

The hardest job kids face today is learning good manners
without seeing any. *Fred Astaire*

■

If we as parents are too busy to listen to our children, how
then can they understand a God who hears? *V. Gilbert
Beers, in* How to Raise Christian Kids in a Non-Christian World

■

Parents who want their children to know God must cultivate their own relationship with God. . . . Happy the child who happens in upon his parent from time to time to see him on his knees, who sees mother and father rising early, or going aside regularly, to keep times with the Lord.   *Larry Christenson*, The Christian Family

■

Love is taught daily by example and by observation, in many little and big ways, in the things that we do for each other, and the things that we let others do for themselves. *Caryl Waller Krueger*, Six Weeks to Better Parenting

■

The imprint of the parent remains forever on the life of the child.   *C.B. Eavey*, 2500 Sentence Sermons

■ ■ ■ ■ ■ ■ ■ ■ ■ ■ ■ ■ ■ ■ ■ ■

HOME-MAKING

Whether a mom is actually in the house full-time, she's absolutely on-the-job full-time! A mother has a unique gift of providing an atmosphere of joy and security for her family, and that kind of home-making is a job that never ends.

Unless the LORD builds the house, its builders labor in vain. *Psalm 127:1*

■

She watches over the affairs of her household
and does not eat the bread of idleness. *Proverbs 31:27*

■

A little house—a house of my own—
Out of the wind's and the rain's way. *Padraic Colum*

■

A hundred men may make an encampment, but it takes a woman to make a home. *Chinese proverb*

■

The wise woman builds her house, but with her own hands the foolish one tears hers down. *Proverbs 14:1*

■

In order to pull together under one roof, all of us need plenty of God's grace. *Ray and Anne Ortlund, in* Parents and Children

■

It's just a small house,
  humble and bare
But you know it's a home
  with all the love there!
Marilyn J. Ferguson

■

Where there is a mother in the house, matters speed well.
A. Bronson Alcott

■

It takes a mother's love
to make a house a home,
A place to be remembered
No matter where we roam.   *Helen Steiner Rice*

■

A suburban mother's role is to deliver children obstetrically
once, and by car forever after.   *Peter deVries*

■

The house of the righteous stands firm.   *Proverbs 12:7*

■

A palace without affection is a poor hovel, and the meanest
hut with love in it is a palace for the soul.   *Robert G. Ingersoll*

■

Lord
Day by day, year by year
Will You remind us

That we have a share in shaping the world
In our town
On our street
In a small yellow house
With glistening white trim.
Ruth Harms Calkin, "Shaping the World," in Lord, I Keep Running
Back to You

■

I am psychologically defeated when I try to take one of
those tests in a magazine to find out if I am a fit house-
wife and mother and I can't find a pencil in a six-room
house. And when I do finally tally up my score, I discover
I am not suited for marriage and motherhood. *Erma Bombeck*, I Lost Everything in the Post-Natal Depression

■

Oh, that our home on earth might be to them the pathway,
the gate to the Father's home in heaven! Blessed Father,
let us and our children be Thine wholly and forever.
Amen. *Andrew Murray*, How to Raise Your Children for Christ

■

Without hearts there is no home. *Lord Byron*

■

Home is the place there's no place like. *Charles Schultz*,
Home Is on Top of a Doghouse

■

Home, sweet home—where each lives for the other, and
all live for God. *T.J. Bach*

■

We shall think of our home and family as His home, the dwelling-place of His holiness. *Andrew Murray*, How to Raise Your Children for Christ

■

'Mid pleasures and palaces
  though we may roam,
Be it ever so humble, there's
  no place like home.
J. Howard Payne

■

Charity begins, but does not end, at home. *Unknown*

■

A home is a place where we find direction. *Gigi Graham Tchividjian*, Thank You, Lord, for My Home

■

Where we love is home.
Home, where our feet may leave but not our hearts.
Oliver Wendell Holmes

■

Whole-life stewardship means putting the purposes of God at the very center of our lives and families.
Tom Sine

■

Home to laughter, home to rest,
Home to those we love the best. . . .

Now the day is done and I
Turn to hear a welcoming cry.
Love is dancing at the door,
I am safe at home once more.
Unknown

■

When there is room in the heart, there is room in the
house.   *Danish proverb*

■

To be happy at home is the ultimate result of all ambition.
Unknown

■

For every home, a cornerstone
That keeps the structure strong,
The home fires burning warm and bright
With cheerfulness and song,
Whene'er you lay a cornerstone,
It holds a precious treasure;
It is a mother's heart of love
Whose worth no man can measure.
Eleanor Fiock

■

Home is not a way station; it is a profession of faith in
life.   *Sol Chaniles*, The New Civility

■

The real art of living is beginning where you are.   *Unknown*

■

She gets up while it is still dark;
   she provides food for her family.
Proverbs 31:15

■

There are only two lasting bequests we can hope to give
our children. One of these is roots; the other wings.
Hodding Carter

■

A little girl, asked where her home was, replied, "Where
Mother is."   *Keith L. Brooks*, The Cream Book: Sentence Sermons

■

Home is where they send your bills.   *Charles Schultz,* Home
Is on Top of a Doghouse

■

To be happy at home is the ultimate result of all ambition;
the end to which every enterprise and labor tends and of
which every desire prompts the prosecution.   *Johnson*

■

The beauty of the house is order:
The blessing of the house is contentment:
The glory of the house is hospitality:
The crown of the house is godliness.
Fireplace motto

■

Home is where the heart is.   *Unknown*

Nor need we power or splendor,
   Wide hall or lordly dome;
The good, the true, the tender,
   These form the wealth of home.

Mrs. Hale

Home is the place where the great are small and the small
are great.   *Robert C. Savage*, Pocket Quips

■

A good laugh is sunshine in a house.   *Thackeray*

■

The best way to keep children home is to make the home atmosphere pleasant—and let the air out of the tires.
Dorothy Parker

■

Childish voices free from care,
Sweet rest in the evening's gloam.
'Tis here treasures are waiting—
Carved deep in the heart and home.
Mamie Osburn Odum

■

Home is where you want to go after a hard day.   *Charles Schultz*, Home Is on Top of a Doghouse

■

It may sound strange to speak of the relationship between parents and children in terms of hospitality. But it belongs to the center of the Christian message that children are not properties to own or rule over, but gifts to cherish and care for. Our children are our most important guests, who enter into our home, ask for careful attention, stay for awhile, and then leave to follow their own way.   *Henri Nouwen*

■

I am sure that if people had to choose between living where the noise of children never stopped and where it

was never heard, all the good-natured and sound people would prefer the incessant noise to the incessant silence.
George Bernard Shaw, Misalliance

■

She keeps her heart at home, secure
Behind familiar locks that bar
The hurting world. She is so sure
It is at home the real joys are.
She keeps her heart at home to bless
The ones she loves with happiness!
Anne Campbell

■

She sets about her work vigorously;
   her arms are strong for her tasks.
Proverbs 31:17

■

Home is where you can kick off your shoes. *Charles Schultz*, Home Is on Top of a Doghouse

■

I wanted a house that would have four bedrooms for the boys, all of them located some distance from the living room—say in the next county somewhere. *Jean Kerr*, Please Don't Eat the Daisies

■

The best place for a child to learn religious faith is at home, in the bosom of a family where faith is lived and practiced. *Dick Van Dyke*, "Faith, Hope and Hilarity," *in* Ideals

■

If you make children happy now, you will make them happy twenty years hence by the memory of it. *Kate Douglas Wiggin*

■

A house is not a home. *Polly Adler*

■

A happy childhood is one of the best gifts that parents have it in their power to bestow. *Mary Cholmondeley*

■

The strength of a nation, especially of a republican nation, is in the intelligent and well-ordered homes of the people. *Mrs. Sigourney*

■

No nation can be destroyed while it possesses a good home life. *J.G. Holland*

■

Keep the home-fires burning. *Lena Guilbert Ford*

■ ■ ■ ■ ■ ■ ■ ■ ■ ■ ■ ■ ■ ■ ■

A FEELING OF FAMILY

Families give individuals a place to belong, a place to find
out their worth and identity, and a place to live out
the commands of God's Word. Thank goodness for the family!

Unity and diversity. Form and freedom. Togetherness and
individuality. A family. *Edith Schaeffer*, What Is a Family?

■

After all is said and done, the most important part of a
child's background at any time is the love and companion-
ship of his parents. Children will leave their most precious
toys or the most fascinating game for a romp with
Mommy and Daddy. The best gift parents can give
children is themselves. *Annie Laurie von Tun*

■

A happy family is but an earlier heaven. *Sir John Browning*

■

For no apparent reason, other than its functional value, the
refrigerator became the meeting place of the American
suburban family. It also became a frozen message center
where anyone could drop by anytime of the day or night.
The rules of communications via refrigerator were simple:
Don't write with food in your hand. If phone numbers
were illegible, be a sport. Messages left unclaimed over
seven years would be destroyed. *Erma Bombeck*, The Grass
Is Always Greener Over the Septic Tank

■

As you pray together for needs inside and outside your immediate family, concern for other family members increases, joys and sorrows are commonly shared, and faith is built as God sends the answers to prayer. *Joyce Heinrich and Annette LaPlaca*, Making Summer Count

■

Families come in different sizes and ages and varieties and colors. What families have in common the world around is that they are the place where people learn who they are and how to be that way. *Jean Illsley Clarke*, Self-Esteem: A Family Affair

■

In your standard issue family . . . there are parents and there are children. The way you know which are which, aside from certain size and age differences and despite any behavior similarities, is that the parents are the bossy ones. *Delia Ephron*, Funny Sauce

■

Family is comfort in grief and joy in time spent together. *Unknown*

■

When the parents are becoming what God wants them to be, and the parents and children are spending a lot of time in their house together being a family, then the house becomes a home, and the home becomes an incubator for ideals, virtues, and visions. *Anne Ortlund*, Disciplines of the Home

■

All happy families resemble one another; every unhappy family is unhappy in its own way. *Leo Tolstoy*

■

Large family, quick help. *Serbian proverb*

■

We grow our first and deepest roots within family and home; strong positive feelings about ourselves and firm emotional ties to others will anchor us in life, nourish our security, and permit us to weather successfully the adversities of our existence. *Bruno Bettelheim,* A Good Enough Parent

■

There is no failure that can alter the course of human events more than failing a family. *Eleanor McGovern*

■

There are no perfect families. *Kevin Leman*

■

If you aim to have a perfect family, you will be sorely disappointed. But you can create a strong family where the members respect each other, are loyal to one another, and enjoy being together. *Judson Swihart, in* Parents and Children

■

The family. We were a strange little band of characters trudging through life sharing diseases and toothpaste, coveting one another's desserts, hiding shampoo, borrowing money, locking each other out of our rooms, inflicting pain and kissing to heal it in the same instant, loving, laughing, defending, and trying to figure out the common thread that bound us all together. *Erma Bombeck*, Family: The Ties That Bind . . . and Gag!

■

The family begins in a commitment of love. *Joseph and Lois Bird,* To Live as Family

■

Your family—whatever the combination of humans under your roof—is a mystery, a marvel, a wonder. God has put you together, and things are happening in you and between you from day to day, from moment to moment. . . . God is powerfully at work. *Anne Ortlund*, Disciplines of the Home

■

There is no such thing as Society. There are individual men and women, and there are families. *Margaret Thatcher*

■

How does family love happen? "Line upon line, precept upon precept," a little here, some there, your example, your guidance, your teaching, your prayers—little by little, children are conformed to Christ's image. *Joyce Heinrich*, Making Summer Count

■

Where could we better invest for the future than in our families? *Richard Evans,* An Open Road

■

Our most basic instinct is not for survival but for family. Most of us would give our own life for the survival of a family member, yet we lead our daily life too often as if we take our family for granted. *Paul Pearshall*, The Power of the Family

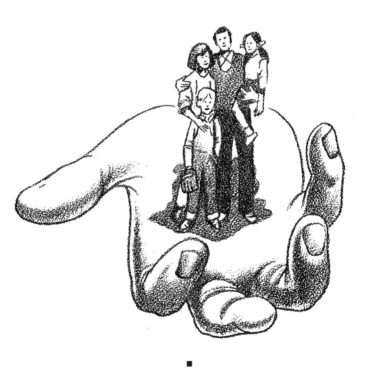

■

The family is God's idea, part of his loving plan for human well-being and joy. *Maxine Hancock*, Creative, Confident Children

■

Whatever is great and good in the institutions and usages of mankind is an application of sentiments that have drawn their first nourishment from the soil of the family. *Felix Adler*

■

Love is the first and most crucial ingredient for a balanced, harmonious family life. If love is freely given and freely accepted with no strings attached, individual freedom and responsibility can develop. *Kay Kuzma*, Prime-Time Parenting

■

Turn the hearts of the parents to the children, and the hearts of the children to the parents; and so enkindle fervent charity among us all, that we may be evermore kindly affectioned with brotherly love. *Episcopal Prayer Book*

■

I am the family face;
Flesh perishes, I live on,
Projecting trait and trace
Through time to times anon,
And leaping from place to place
Over oblivion.
Thomas Hardy, "Heredity"

■

The family is a school for relationships. Along with providing food, shelter, and clothing, the family teaches its members how to get along with each other. . . . Growing up in a family, the most important lesson you learn is how to build ties with other people. *Mary Durkin*, Making Your Family Work

■

Responsibility must be at the heart of loving within the family. *Joseph and Lois Bird*, To Live as Family

■

Your family is unique. When God hand-picked your one-of-a-kind spouse and your one-of-a-kind children, he gave you the bond of family. *Joyce Heinrich and Annette LaPlaca*, Making Summer Count

■

"I do think that families are the most beautiful things in all the world!" *Jo March in* Little Women, *Louisa May Alcott*

■

Life is short, and we never have too much time for gladdening the hearts of those who are traveling the dark way with us. Oh, be swift to love! Make haste to be kind! *Henri Amiel*

■

God made us a family.
We need one another.
We love one another.
We work together.
We play together.
Together we use God's Word.

Together we grow in Christ.
Together we love all men.
Together we serve God.
Together we hope in heaven.
These are our hopes and ideals;
Help us to attain them, O God.
Through Jesus Christ our Lord, Amen.
The Christian Family Standard, Lutheran Church, Missouri Synod

■

The family that prays together stays together. *Al Scalpon, for the Roman Catholic Family Rosary Crusade*

■

It must be said that we can have joy, and therefore will it, only as we give it to others. *Karl Barth*

■

Nobody's family can hang out the sign, "Nothing the matter here." *Chinese proverb*

■

Some people think that the amateurishness of family life is the most widely distributed human beauty. *Harold Brodkey, "A Largely Oral History of My Mother"*

■

A family is a unit composed not only of children but of man, woman, an occasional animal, and the common cold. *Ogden Nash*

■

To the family—that dear octopus from whose tentacles we never quite escape, nor, in our inmost hearts, ever quite wish to.   *Dodie Smith*

■

If I am committed to making my family strong and happy, then I won't collapse when pressures come along. Instead, I'll stick in there and work at building a healthy family. *Gary R. Collins, in* Parents and Children

■

Finally, all of you, live in harmony with one another; be sympathetic, love as brothers, be compassionate and humble.   *1 Peter 3:8*

■ ■ ■ ■ ■ ■ ■ ■ ■ ■ ■ ■ ■ ■ ■

A WOMAN OF GOD

With all the demands of family and home-life, it's hard for a mother to find time to consider who she is before the Lord. Take some time out for yourself; renew parenting and personal goals.

A woman who fears the LORD is to be praised. *Proverbs 31:30*

■

Life is a series of peak-and-valley experiences. The good times don't last forever, but neither do the bad. . . . The struggles and the wear and tear are worth it when every so often, just when you need it most, your son or daughter gives you a quick hug and says, "You're the best mom in the whole world!" *Bobbie Reed*, Single Mothers Raising Sons

■

True strength is delicate. *Louise Nevelson*

■

Labors of love are light. Routine is a hard master. Love much, and you can do much. Impossibilities disappear when zeal is fervent. *Unknown*

■

Nothing is so strong as gentleness, nothing as gentle as true strength. *St. Francis de Sales*

■

The secret of staying young is to live honestly, eat slowly, and lie about your age. *Lucille Ball*

■

Be strong and courageous. *Joshua 1:9*

■

Cheerfulness means a contented spirit; a pure heart, a kind and loving disposition; it means humility and charity, a generous appreciation of others, and a modest opinion of self. *Thackeray*

■

A kindhearted woman gains respect. *Proverbs 11:16*

■

Modesty: the gentle art of enhancing your charm by pretending not to be aware of it. *Oliver Herford*

■

A woman whose smile is open and whose expression is glad has a kind of beauty no matter what she wears. *Anne Roiphe, "The Beauty Trap," in* Family Circle

■

Acknowledge the God of your father, and serve him with wholehearted devotion and with a willing mind, for the LORD searches every heart and understands every motive behind the thoughts. If you seek him, he will be found by you; but if you forsake him, he will reject you forever. *1 Chronicles 28:9*

■

Fill me with Your love
Your radiance
Your wisdom and power.
Make my life the proof
Of the truth I proclaim.
I am not content, dear Lord
Simply to impart information.
I long to behold transformation.
Ruth Harms Calkin, "Transformation," Lord, I Keep Running Back to You

■

Every calling is great when greatly pursued. *Unknown*

■

In recent years, women have experienced more freedom . . . freedom to develop gifts, pursue dreams,
and become leaders in areas that used to be off-limits.
R. Ruth Barton, Women Like Us

■

Pray every day for your children. This is an area where
Christian parents don't have an option. *Dick Hagstrom, in*
Parents and Children

■

The people I know who truly like themselves as persons,
apart from their roles in life as husband, wife, parent, or
job-holder, are those who have learned to be honest with
themselves and who to some degree understand themselves. . . . Honesty with oneself, with God, and with
one's fellow man is the first all-important step in spiritual
and emotional growth. *Cecil G. Osborne,* The Art of Learning
to Love Yourself

■

The Greeks believed beauty was to be found in harmony,
in dignity, and women who accept themselves in all the
stages of life achieve that balance. *Anne Roiphe, "The
Beauty Trap," in* Family Circle

■

I'm tired of all this nonsense about beauty being only skin
deep. That's deep enough. What do you want—an
adorable pancreas? *Jean Kerr,* How I Got to Be Perfect

■

Like a gold ring in a pig's snout is a beautiful woman who shows no discretion.
Proverbs 11:22

■

A woman's hopes are woven on sunbeams; a shadow annihilates them.   *George Eliot*

■

Grace was in all her steps, heaven in her eye.
In every gesture dignity and love.
John Milton

■

The secret of being lovely is being unselfish.   *Holland*

■

The highest pinnacle of the spiritual life is not joy in
unbroken sunshine but absolute and undoubting trust in
the love of God. *A.W. Thorold*

■

His divine power has given us everything we need for life
and godliness through our knowledge of him who called
us by his own glory and goodness. Through these he has
given us his very great and precious promises. *2 Peter 1:3-4*

■ ■ ■ ■ ■ ■ ■ ■ ■ ■ ■ ■ ■ ■ ■

INDEX